Katrina and the Unforgettable
Mississippi Autumn on Bluebird Hill

A true story about Autumn 2005 on the farm in Southern Mississippi

Katrina and the Unforgettable

MISSISSIPPI AUTUMN ON BLUEBIRD HILL

A true story about Autumn 2005 on the farm in Mississippi with Mama B, Papa Doc, and a dog named Bo

by
Billie Remson

Hot Chocolate Books

A Division of

Word Association Publishers
205 Fifth Avenue
Tarentum, Pennsylvania 15084

Copyright © 2006 by Billie Remson.

All rights reserved. No part of this book may be used or reproduced in any manner whatsoever without written permission of the author.

Printed in the United States of America.

Softback:
ISBN 10: 1-59571-121-X
ISBN 13: 978-1-59571-121-2

Hardback:
ISBN 10: 1-59571-158-9
ISBN 13: 978-1-5971-158-8

Library of Congress Control Number: 2006922118

Hot Chocolate Books
A division of Word Association Publishers
205 Fifth Avenue
Tarentum, Pennsylvania 15084
www.wordassociation.com

Acknowledgements

Francine Costello, my Editor. Her expertise refining my books and encouragement along the way.

Kym Garraway, my Illustrator. Her God-given talent and the concept to write about Bluebird Hill.

With my sincere thanks and love to both, *Billie*

Also by Billie Remson

A Mississippi Spring On Bluebird Hill

A Mississippi Summer On Bluebird Hill

A Mississippi Winter On Bluebird Hill

*"There is a time for everything
and a season for every activity."* Ecclesiastes 3:1a

Holy Bible New International Version, Holman Bible Publishers, Colorado Springs, CO

AUTUMN

The season of the year between summer and winter. Autumn, also called fall, is a season of maturity, a time of preparation.

It's nearing the end of August—a time when we can't help but dream about the cooler weather with the coming of autumn. For much of the summer, Mississippi has endured the usual intense heat and humidity. Bluebird Hill and all its inhabitants have been doing their best to stay cool. Most of the time, staying cool can be fun—swimming, boating, or lounging in the deep shade of our lovely old trees are favorites with us. Even getting soaked by a surprise afternoon shower while strolling along Rabbit Run Road can be a delight on a hot Mississippi day. But when the end of August rolls around, there is always that yearning for the crisp joys of autumn on Bluebird Hill.

Bluebird Hill is the name of the farm that Mama B and Papa Doc share with their Shetland Sheepdog named Bo. The farm is located in south central Mississippi between the towns of Tylertown and McComb.

Today there is a whisper of a northern breeze, making it a perfect day for Mama B and Papa Doc to take a ninety mile drive west of Bluebird Hill to historic Natchez, Mississippi. Natchez is the oldest civilized settlement on the Mississippi River. This beautiful town sits on large hills overlooking the mighty Mississippi River. Natchez is famous for its gracious homes and warm friendly people. The city is preparing for its annual fall pilgrimage in October. Natchez has more antebellum (that means they were built before the Civil War) homes than any other place in the United States. Many of these homes are open for visitors during the fall pilgrimage.

Mama B and Papa Doc love strolling the shaded streets of Natchez, enjoying the beauty of the gracious old houses and the views of the river. Before they head for home, they will have an authentic southern dinner in one of the city's many good restaurants.

They'll probably enjoy it a little more than they should and that will mean Mama B will have to decline Papa Doc's kind offer of white chocolate bread pudding or Mississippi mud cake for dessert.

On the drive back to Bluebird Hill, Mama B and Papa Doc talk about their plans for this autumn. There is much work to getting a farm ready for the cooler months and Papa Doc already has a long to-do list. Mama B has a list as well, but hers includes a few things that are more fun than work. The whole family looks forward to the traditions she has established for autumn. This is a favorite time on Bluebird Hill but neither Papa Doc nor Mama B can guess that this coming autumn will be one that will never be forgotten.

When Mama B and Papa Doc return to their little farm from their day trip, they notice a change in the weather. The pleasant, northerly breeze that they have been enjoying has changed. Now the air, like hot breath coming from the south, is warm and tropical. The sun has disappeared and the clouds are low. The wind chimes hanging on the porch and in the trees on Bluebird Hill have changed from their gentle, tinkling to an insistent clanging, as the warm wind pushes harder and harder. Mama B and Papa Doc need no noisy reminders that this is a sure sign of a coming storm—maybe even a hurricane. They are well aware that the Gulf of Mexico, which is only one hundred miles away, has a history of dangerous hurricanes from June through November.

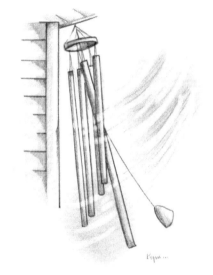

FRIDAY, AUGUST 26, 2005

Everyone knows Mama B, always a cautious and careful person, is even more so during hurricane season, when she constantly monitors the weather reports. A quick check of the Weather Channel on television and Mama B discovers that an actual hurricane, named Katrina, has indeed entered the Gulf of Mexico. Katrina is being called an especially dangerous hurricane and the reporters are saying it could grow into a monstrous storm as it churns its way toward Louisiana and Mississippi.

The vibrant, colorful city of New Orleans, Louisiana, is below sea level. This means the city was built on land that is lower than the ocean. New Orleans is Papa Doc's beloved hometown. Experts have warned for years that a big storm could hit it and cause dangerous flooding in the city.

"Looks like our luck is running out, Papa Doc, this one is huge," says a worried Mama B as she sits in front of the television gently patting Bo's head, "and they're saying that this giant-of-a storm could grow even larger."

"We have a lot of outside work to do to prepare Bluebird Hill" says the always calm and practical, Papa Doc. "This big old Katrina could bring a lot of nasty wind and rain for the farm."

As they study the weather map on the TV screen, Mama B and Papa Doc can see that Katrina is so large that by the time it touches the southern most part of Louisiana, they will be feeling its mighty force on Bluebird Hill, almost two hundred miles away.

SATURDAY, AUGUST 27, 2005

It's very early morning but Mama B and Papa Doc are already in Tylertown preparing for the storm. Papa Doc first fills the truck with gas and gas cans with extra gasoline. Once the storm hits, gasoline will be much needed and in short supply.

Little downtown Tylertown with its one lonesome red light, is in the midst of a major traffic jam. Since Tylertown is north of New Orleans, people from Louisiana have headed that way for safety and are now clogging every street and roadway. Some families are traveling in two, three, and four-car caravans, loaded down with pets, medicine, documents, treasured family heirlooms and photographs—anything and everything that is important and essential is packed in tightly. To add to the confusion, like Mama B and Papa Doc, almost everyone who lives in or near Tylertown is in town to pick up supplies before the storm hits.

After several stops and purchases, Mama B is happy to end up at her favorite place—the grocery store. The store is crowded and the lines are long. Mama B chats with other shoppers. Everyone is talking about how they are preparing for the storm. Mama B is running into so many friends and neighbors that Papa Doc finally has to hurry her along. There is still much to buy and he's anxious to get back to the farm.

At the top of the list are batteries for the

flashlights and radios and more food that can be kept without refrigeration. Sometimes, hurricanes blow down wires and electricity and phone service can be off for a week or longer. Papa Doc has loaded extra bags of ice into the grocery cart to fill an ice chest, which will serve as their temporary refrigerator. The ice will be stored in the freezer until it is needed.

Back on Bluebird Hill, Mama B fills empty gallon plastic jugs with water and places them in the freezer along with the extra ice. The thermostat on the refrigerator and freezer is turned all the way down. They want all the food in the freezer to freeze hard and stay frozen as long as possible, even after the electricity goes out. The ice in the jugs will be used to keep the whole refrigerator cold. Melted ice in the jug can be used later for drinking water, if needed.

Next Mama B takes down the wind chimes and the American flag. She and Papa Doc work together on the porch as they lower the swing, put it away, and push all the porch furniture against the wall of the porch.

SUNDAY, AUGUST 28, 2005

The wind has gained more strength over night and is pushing the dense, dark clouds across the sky. It's hard to imagine that the sun is actually shining high above the angry, churning gloom.

As usual, Mama B and Papa Doc attend

church services. It is a comfort to join their friends and neighbors in prayer for everyone's safety from the terrible storm that's headed their way.

After church, it's back to the grocery store to stock up on more food. Mama B will buy fried chicken, sandwich meat, fresh bread, and canned tuna. When they get home, she will boil lots of good farm-fresh eggs. The eggs will make a fine source of protein and they will be wonderful in tuna salad. Mama B will also make certain that she gets Papa Doc his favorite cookies.

Once back on Bluebird Hill, Mama B and Papa Doc call all their children to make certain that they and the grandchildren will be in a safe place with plenty of food and water, when Katrina hits. All assure them that they are well-prepared and not to worry.

Late Sunday afternoon Mama B takes the bird feeders down. She has given the birds all day to fill their energetic bodies with seeds before they settle into the woods to take shelter from the storm. Papa Doc has returned from the pond where he pulled the boat ashore and tied it to a tree. Now, he is taking down their grandchildren's tire swing that is attached with a rope to a limb of Fritz's old oak tree. Fritz peeks out the top of his nest to check out the action below, as the wind blows the old oak tree and sways his nest back and forth. These early puffs from Katrina will most likely rock Fritz to sleep.

Mama B now rushes off to consider what is to be done with her beloved chickens. The Bluebird Hill farmhouse was built on a cinder block foundation that is elevated about three feet off the ground under the living room. Mama B thinks that this space might be the perfect storm shelter for her chickens. Papa Doc is not too sure about chickens under the house. Besides, he reminds Mama B that the place where she is proposing to house the chickens is close to the lovely, strong, underground storm cellar he built for them under their bedroom. The storm cellar has easy access using a spiral staircase from the bedroom. Papa Doc is worried about the noise the chickens will make. But Mama B convinces him that the chickens won't be the tiniest bit of trouble and she's certain this is best for the welfare of her little Bantams.

The feeders and water containers are placed under the house first. Then, while Papa Doc continues to secure things around the farm, it's back to the chicken house where Mama B catches the chickens and brings them—four and five at a time—to their new protected home where they will spend the next two or three days.

Finally, Mama B takes care of one last preparation. She fills the bath tubs and the washing machine with water. This water isn't for drinking. They have plenty of drinking water in containers. This water in the tubs and washing machine is for keeping clean and fresh. A big storm, like the one that appears to be coming, can shut down all services. So it pays to be prepared.

Papa Doc has done all he can to secure the farm from the coming storm. He and Mama B are both tired from all the hard work. At about eight on Sunday evening, the first bands of rain begin a noisy dance on the tin roof of the farmhouse.

After what may be their last hot-cooked meal for a while, Mama B and Papa Doc prepare for bed. But Mama B, the weather worrier in the family, just has to check the Weather Channel one last time. At this late hour, they are reporting that the eye or center of the storm could come ashore south of the city of New

Orleans some time around dawn tomorrow. Experts are worried that the giant storm could cause serious flooding in New Orleans.

"Mama B," calls Papa Doc, "let's try to get some sleep tonight and not worry about Katrina until tomorrow."

"You're right—tomorrow will surely be a rough day on Bluebird Hill," Mama B tells the never-excited-over-weather Papa Doc, as she slips into their bed, with Bo curled-up nearby on the carpet. A tired Mama B says one more prayer for all who are in the path of Katrina and takes comfort in the thought of her little Bantam hens and roosters snug and safe under the house.

MONDAY, AUGUST 29, 2005

It is four o'clock in the morning when Mama B awakens. Papa Doc is still sleeping—sound as ever. The wind is howling like a hound dog. The bands of rain are pounding hard on Bluebird Hill. Katrina has arrived. Mama B turns on the lamp and the television so that she can watch the Weather Channel while she brews a pot of coffee. Nervous and concerned about her loved ones, Mama B watches and listens for updates. She learns that in about two hours, the eye of the hurricane will be near the mouth of the Mississippi River just south of New Orleans. Forecasters are warning that the giant storm will cause wind and water surges in New Orleans and along the Gulf Coast. A surge means that the ocean will rise and come crashing up on land.

They are also predicting that the eye or center of the storm could come as close as fifty miles from Bluebird Hill later today. That is too close for Mama B. She is thankful they have a storm shelter under the house. And she is thankful that the storm shelter is nicely separated from the space under the house where the chickens are staying. She smiles as she admits to herself that her little family of Bantams is indeed a noisy bunch.

Worry over the storm is making Mama B want

to start nibbling. *Oh, maybe breakfast since it's getting close to daylight.* She prepares a good farm-fresh egg, toast, with a little blueberry jelly, and another cup of coffee. Papa Doc is still sound asleep. Bo is uneasy but calm. He lies down at Mama B's feet as she sits in the recliner, eating her breakfast and not missing a single word of the weather update.

At six o'clock, the bulb in the lamp next to her chair starts to blink and, as if saying goodbye—off goes the electricity. The house is dark and quiet now except for the pounding rain on the tin roof and the screaming wind outside. And, oh yes, the roosters under the house are crowing for all they are worth. Okay, quiet is not exactly the right word to describe the Bluebird Hill farmhouse.

Mama B, with her trusty flashlight, has turned on two battery operated radios, one to listen to the national weather service and the other to hear the reports from the local radio station. *It is a good thing we bought all those extra batteries.*

When the gray and stormy dawn breaks, Mama B looks out of the kitchen window and watches as Mama Cow and her little calf, Paprika, graze near the pond. Katrina is bearing down on Bluebird Hill and Mama B would feel better if the cows would take shelter in the woods as they usually do. The rain begins blowing sideways in the powerful wind. As Mama B continues watching, she sees Kahoe the bull approach the cows and, as if he has given an order, they form a straight line behind him. Once organized, he bravely leads the way into the wind, with his head down. What a sight it is! Kahoe the bull in front; then The Mower, her heifer, Midnight; Mama Cow and her calf; and finally little Paprika, running to bring up the rear. Kahoe, solemn and calm, leads them in their usual walking path and soon they disappear into the safety of the pine tree thicket.

Thank you, Lord for giving animals such wisdom.

There are times when the punishing wind and rain slacks off as the sky lightens. During one of these breaks, Mama B feeds Bo and lets him go outside for a brief run.

Soon there is another band of howling wind and heavy rain, and it starts all over again. Limbs and mistletoe blow across the yard, needles from the pine trees are thrust against the windows and stick there. Bo is happy to be safe and snug back inside the farmhouse.

Papa Doc awakens too late for a nice hot breakfast since the electricity is already off, so he enjoys a bowl of cold cereal and settles into his recliner with a good book. Though Papa Doc sits far enough from the window to protect himself from any possible breaking glass, there is enough daylight to allow him to read. This latest band of punishing wind and rain has sent Mama B and Bo into the storm cellar.

"Papa Doc," calls Mama B, "it's very nice and cozy down here. Would you like to join us until the storm lets up?"

Papa Doc is only steps away from the storm shelter stairway but he declines Mama B's invitation to join her and Bo in the shelter. Though he's always calm and reassuring, Papa Doc likes to keep a watch on things during a storm and so he rarely retreats to the storm cellar, tempting though it is.

Mama B has gone to great pains to make the shelter cheery. She gave it a color theme of red, white and blue and keeps a decorated Christmas tree up all year. These little special touches help to give Mama B courage when the storms come. She thinks about the unique room as she sits in her comfortable chair and tries not to focus too much on the power and might of Katrina. But with the weather radios giving constant updates, it isn't easy to forget that the wind is now sixty-five miles an hour with gusts close to one-hundred miles per hour. Mama B relays the report to Papa Doc, who continues reading his book by the light coming in from the window. From time to time, he takes off his reading glasses, to check on a favorite little oak tree in the front yard and wonders if it is going to survive the massive winds. With each gust the young, fifteen-foot tree leans a little more toward the ground, as the storm savagely strips its branches of leaves.

During another break in the storm, Mama B comes up the stairs, out of the shelter under the bedroom. She is reminded of the groundhog coming out to see his shadow. She would love to see her shadow right now from sunlight beaming in the window. But instead of bright sunlight and a crisp shadow, Mama B faces a dark and angry sky and she notices that several pine trees in the yard have broken off about half way up the trunk.

When Katrina resumes her angry pounding and howling, Mama B returns to the shelter and continues to listen to her radios. Local people are calling in to report trees down across highways and county roads. Some trees have fallen on houses. Downtown Tylertown seems to be taking a hard hit from the powerful storm. Callers are reporting that awnings and roofs from buildings are blowing right down main street, barely missing the town's lone traffic light as it swings wildly in the storm.

Not to be outdone by the din of the storm, the

Bantam roosters, under the house, are still crowing madly. By contrast, the sensible little hens are quietly content. Bo, not normally a lover of storms, is restless but is behaving remarkably well. After all, Mama B is doing enough worrying and praying for everyone on the farm and everywhere else in Katrina's path.

It is early afternoon — Mama B has surfaced again from the shelter. She has been nibbling all morning but hasn't made any preparations for a decent lunch. She dashes to the kitchen and returns to the living room with sandwiches and fruit. While Mama B and Papa Doc eat their lunch, Papa Doc points out that all the trees are leaning to the southeast. That means the storm is passing to the east of Bluebird Hill and the farm is getting the powerful outer-band wind gusts of the storm's core or center. Once lunch is over, Mama B and Bo return to the safety of the storm shelter and again Papa Doc prefers to keep watch above.

The rain is still blowing sideways as the wind roars. Many tornadoes have been reported in the area. It is raining so hard now that Papa Doc can barely see the pond from the front windows. Finally, when the rain slacks between bands, the pond comes into view—gray, swollen, and overflowing as it empties into the spillway and down the valley behind the dam. In this same lull, Mama B climbs the little spiral stairway to join Papa Doc at the window. They are surprised to see that the cows have moved out of the thicket in the woods and are laying on the ground, in the protection of the little valley, at the edge of the pond. There they are safe from the most punishing gusts but more importantly, they are out of danger from the many falling trees and branches, which must have been a terrible hazard when they were in the thicket.

More powerful evidence of how much God loves and cares for his creatures.

Another gust of wind pushes the young oak tree closer to the ground. "That little tree can't take much more of this," says Papa Doc. "I fear it will be uprooted before dark."

While Papa Doc worries about his trees, Mama B is wondering about Fritz and the birds. She feels certain the birds are nestled in the  thickest part of the woods near the farmhouse and Fritz is likely in the very bottom of his drey, or as Mama B calls it, his nest, using his fluffy tail to protect his body. At least his big old oak tree is standing strong in this storm.

Mama B laughs as she hears Rufus' loud crowing coming from under the living room floor. Hewey, Dewey and Lewey join in with their not-yet-perfected crows. The roosters, confused by the day-long darkness, probably believe they are giving their morning wake-up call. *Oh well*, Mama B thinks, *the crowing is a small price to pay for the safety of her brood*. When she sees Papa Doc smiling, she knows he agrees.

Late in the afternoon, as the center of the massive storm moves slowly to the northeastern part of Mississippi, the rain begins to let up. By sunset, the rain has stopped temporarily and there is a little blue sky showing in the west. "It's a blessed sight to see" Mama B tells Papa Doc as they venture out of the farmhouse for the first time that day.

Though the old oak tree where Fritz lives is safe, Mama B and Papa Doc are stunned that one of their other massive oaks is completely uprooted. This sight and other evidence tells them that one of the many tornadoes in the region, may have crashed into Bluebird Hill. "Mama B," admits Papa Doc, "if I had known a tornado was that close to us, I would surely have joined you in the storm cellar."

Though the wind is still kicking up now and again with the return of torrents of rain, the storm is making a slow crawl out of the area. "Tomorrow we will begin to clean-up Katrina's mess," says Papa Doc.

After setting the table with paper plates, paper cups and disposable forks and knives, Mama B invites Papa Doc to sit down to dinner. The meal consists of delicious smoked ribs, baked beans (right out of the can), good garden-fresh sliced tomatoes, stuffed eggs and of course Papa Doc's favorite chocolate chip cookies for dessert. When they give thanks, Mama B and Papa Doc remember the many who are going without on this difficult evening. They are stricken by news reports of the terrible losses in New Orleans and along the coast. They pray that their family is safe. With telephone lines down and cell phones out of service, both are relying on their deep faith and trust in the Lord.

When bedtime comes, Mama B and Papa Doc take refreshing sponge baths using the water reserved in the bathtubs. Bo, who usually curls up on the soft carpet, chooses a cool spot on the wood floor. All of the screened windows and doors are opened wide and the temperature is actually quite tolerable. Again, during prayers, they offer thanks for their blessings and angels to watch over their loved ones and all who are suffering this dark night.

The next morning, as soon as Mama B and Papa Doc can get out of the house, Papa Doc cranks up his old blue tractor. He has placed a board down the trunk of the little oak tree that took such a beating in the storm. Mama B holds the board in place, between the tree and the tractor, as Papa Doc pushes the oak as straight as he can with the old tractor. Papa Doc then hammers a steel rod into the ground and ties a rope from the tree to the rod to brace the young tree. Hopefully the root system will find its way back in the ground again and the sun will help it straighten.

Mama B puts the bird feeders back up—though there is neither the sound or the sight of a single bird. *Where have the dear little creatures gone*, Mama B worries.

Papa Doc starts to work sawing one of the huge pine trees that was uprooted. Next he will tackle all the tree limbs and trash that is scattered in the yard. The putt-putt of the tractor and whine of the chain saw will be an almost constant sound for many days.

Finally, Mama B puts the chickens back in the chicken house. They fly, jump, cluck, cackle and crow to show their happiness to be back in their own home.

Late in the afternoon, after a hectic day of hard work, Mama B rests for a moment on the porch. It is during these quiet times that worries about the family, the tragic flood in New Orleans, and the horrible losses along the Mississippi coast fill her mind and heart. Mama B's thoughts are very far away when Papa Doc sits down beside her and asks, "Mama B, what did you have on when the electricity went off?" Like someone awakened from a dream, Mama B is puzzled by Papa Doc's strange question. "Why my long pink nightgown, of course! Why are you asking me that?"

Papa Doc looks at her with his brown beaded eyes and grins. "No, Mama B, I don't mean what were you wearing, what I mean is, did you have on—the television, the lamp, the radio?" They both laugh heartily—a laugh that was needed after these hectic and stressful days.

That evening, Mama B and Papa Doc open the ice chest again to see what to have for dinner. The food in the ice chest doesn't look quite as appetizing on this, the second day, but they are grateful for what they have. They settle on fried chicken, a sandwich and a cookie. Since they have almost no water pressure from the community water system, after dinner Mama B and Papa Doc each enjoy a good, brief and very cold bath using the water Mama B had reserved in their bath tubs. They each had their own tub and Mama B warns Papa Doc not to drain the water when he finishes his bath because he may be using the same bathwater for a few days yet. But used bathwater is nothing compared to the radio's descriptions of the unspeakable destruction Katrina has caused in the whole Gulf region. The coastal areas have the most serious damage and injuries. And though their community has little running water, no electricity or phone service, trees toppled over on houses and blocking roads, and many missing roofs, everyone, so far, seems to be safe.

The tolerable temperatures of the previous day have now been replaced by a heavy, tropical heat and all of the wide-open windows in the farmhouse do little to alleviate it. *Mustn't think about our heavenly air conditioner or the soft hum of the ceiling fan,* Mama B tells herself. *We have to be grateful for the roof over our heads.* And so she focuses on being thankful.

After three days of hard work putting the pieces back together on the farm, Mama B and Papa Doc, like thousands upon thousands of people in their region, are tired and hot. They have still not been able to talk with their children or grandchildren since before the storm. With most of the roads still blocked by fallen trees, they can't leave the farm to visit neighbors. They aren't listening to the radio as much anymore because they want to conserve their batteries. The temperature is in the high eighties during the day and the nights are long, hot, and very dark. The news reports say that electrical power isn't likely to be turned on for another three to four weeks. That's a lot longer than expected and Mama B is worried about losing everything they have in the freezer. Both Mama B and Papa Doc agree that the food in the ice chest does not taste as good as it once did and they are getting tired of used bath water. But from the bits of news they hear on the radio, they have little to complain about, and spend much time praying for those many people who were not so fortunate.

Mama B and Papa Doc are sitting on the front porch listening to a magnificent frog concert performed by the multitude who make their home in the pond. The charming dance by the fireflies, on this humid night, is made all the more enchanting by the absence of the moon. Mama B is fanning her face with her watermelon-shaped hand fan when, suddenly, Bo's bark alerts them that a vehicle is coming down the gravel road.

"Who could possibly get through the blocked roads to the farm, in the darkness of the night?" Papa Doc says.

Since they are sitting outside, on the front porch, in their coolest night clothes, Papa Doc rushes inside to grab his pants, and hurries back out to meet the visitors. Mama B is using a flashlight to find a robe when the headlights of the vehicle come to a stop close to the side porch where Papa Doc is standing. Now they can see the outline of a pick-up truck, pulling a loaded trailer. The voices of their son-in-law Kevin and his friend Chris bring tears to Mama B's eyes and a big smile to Papa Doc's face. The two men drove two hours to bring supplies and make sure Mama B and Papa Doc are safe. This was their first opportunity to make the one hundred mile trip south to Bluebird Hill. With no telephone service, electricity, little gasoline and nearly all roads impassable, they had no choice but to wait and hope that all would be well.

Using a chain saw, the men explain, they

hacked their way up the main road to the lane leading to Bluebird Hill. Their trailer is loaded with a generator, cans of gas, bottled water, and ice chests filled with ice and fresh food. But best of all, the men bring news that their family is safe. What a great show of love, family unity, and friendship!

That night, with the ceiling fan powered by the generator blowing a cool breeze across their bed, Mama B and Papa give thanks for their angels in a pick-up truck. Now, because of the generator, their refrigerator and freezer are humming again and they have even been able to enjoy the happy glow of an honest-to-goodness lamp.

Fritz, the unusual squirrel with the unusual name, is spotted in his old oak tree just four days after the hurricane. Shortly thereafter Bluebird Hill is blessed with the return of birds and the eerie silence of the early days after Katrina is broken by their beautiful chirps and songs. The mooing of the cows, crowing of the roosters, clucking of the hens, and the glorious symphony of songbirds brings Bluebird Hill to life once again.

After two weeks Mama B and Papa Doc celebrate the return of the electricity and water. Now it is time for them to begin helping others. Large transport trucks from all over the United States are delivering supplies to the local churches and community centers for distribution throughout the region. It is good to get away from the farm and join their friends and neighbors to help unload, organize, and distribute these much-needed supplies.

The community around Bluebird Hill is a place very different from what it was before the storm. Many in the area have extended family or friends still living with them. Blue tarps cover the tops of houses where roofs were blown off. This is not the usual Mississippi autumn scene with its bright fall flowers and leaves beginning to turn. So much of the foliage has been torn away by the storm that many trees, if standing at all, are bare and Katrina's vicious winds have taken almost every flower.

On the way back and forth through the county roads to Tylertown, Mama B notices make-shift signs directing people to the St. Francis Animal Shelter near the farm. One afternoon she decides to follow the signs to see what is going on at St. Francis. What she finds there are hundreds of animals that have been rescued from the flooded neighborhoods of New Orleans and surrounding areas. Mama B always knew that the St. Francis Animal Sanctuary was near Bluebird Hill, but she has no idea that since the storm, they had joined forces with Best Friends Animal Society from Utah. Now St. Francis is a relocation hub for the thousands of animals rescued from the flood in New Orleans. St. Francis had the space and Best Friends, the many volunteers from all over the United States, anxious to come and help.

As she drives through the shelter grounds, she is amazed at the display of car license plates. *Look at how Katrina has affected people everywhere!* Many drove long distances to help the animals. There are cars from Canada, Utah, Vermont, Colorado, California, New Jersey, Arizona, Washington, Pennsylvania—Mama B finally loses count. Now she notices that little tents are scattered across the grounds. Clothes that have been hand washed are hanging on a fence to dry. Portable toilets and makeshift showers put a smile on Mama B's face. *Lord, bless these good people who have given up all the comforts of their homes to come here and work.* She watches and listens as dedicated volunteers give loving new names to the once-suffering and frightened, dogs and cats.

Mama B stops by the kitchen to see what is going on there. She wants to meet the cook responsible for feeding the seventy or so, mostly volunteer, workers. To her surprise, she finds that they are cooking outside on a gas grill and portable gas burners. They do not have a stove. Mama B cannot imagine trying to cook for this many people without a stove or an oven.

On her drive out of the facility, Mama B weeps for the animals who were once beloved pets. She is also heartbroken for the pet owners who are enduring so many hardships along with the loss of the animals they had to leave behind. Mama B knows she will never forget the frightened looks of these rescued dogs and cats, so bedraggled as they are unloaded at the shelter. But as she considers the situation, her tears turn into a smile. Mama B knows that she is privileged to witness these acts of kindness. Every effort is being made to give each animal as much comfort and care as is possible. While the daily temperatures are still in the nineties, the dogs, in particular, are kept cool with electric fans and the exercise yards are shaded with tarps. But not one of the workers has any such luxury though no one seems to mind a bit. When she thinks about her visits with the animals who have been at the shelter for awhile, she knows that the love is working its magic. Dogs greet her with bright eyes and wagging tails and the purring of cats tells Mama B all she needs to know.

But Mama B being Mama B wants very much to do something to help. In a flash, she decides her mission will be to take care of the caretakers. Soon she is making daily visits to the shelter, which is just across the woods from Bluebird Hill. Mama B has made it her job to bring the wonderful workers fresh baked goodies she makes with her farm-fresh eggs. Some days it's her delicious sugar cookies, sometimes it's devil's food cake with chocolate fudge pecan frosting, or pineapple cake with pineapple icing, or old-fashioned tea cakes. Soon Mama B is famous in the shelter community—known as the *dessert lady*. As time goes by, some volunteers say they heard about Mama B and her deliveries even before arriving at the shelter.

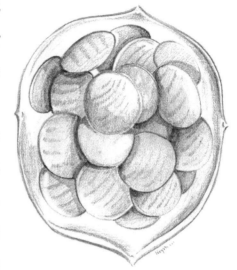

The visits to the shelter are the highlight of Mama B's busy day. The smiles on the workers' faces as she brings them her fresh-baked goodies is helping her to cope with the sadness brought about by all the suffering and destruction caused by Katrina.

Mama B knows that by bringing these good people a little something to look forward to each day she is helping them to stay strong and happy so that they can continue helping the animals. And everyone knows how much love and joy those animals bring to our lives. It's really beautiful the way good works and selfless acts bring about more good works and selfless acts.

Though Katrina has surely made this a challenging autumn Mama B and Papa Doc, like so many in the region, are grateful for every sign that promises a return to normal life. As always, it's a joy watching the antics of Fritz, the unusual squirrel with the unusual name, who lives in the big oak tree beside the farmhouse. Rufus the rooster, the little hens, Cream, and Goldie, their little ones, Sugar, Spice, Lewey, Dewey and Hewey are content in their fenced yards. Papa Doc has built another chicken house and has added two more chicken yards. The chicken yards have little trap doors attached to the fence. The door can be left open or can be closed when the chickens need to be separated. The biddies that Cream and Goldie hatched in the spring are all grown up now and are enjoying all this new scratching room.

Mama B has lots of pine straw to rake since

hurricane Katrina left the farm. She is placing it on the ground in the chicken yard and chuckles as she watches Rufus discover a bug in it. He sends up a food alert sound and all the chickens rush over to him. Usually, when he does this, one of the little hens takes the prize in her mouth and runs with it. All the other chickens run behind her, trying to take it away. If she's clever, she will quickly swallow the catch and end the chase.

Many other animals living in the woods come out to see what is happening on Bluebird Hill. Mama B especially likes the rabbit family. Mrs. Rabbit raised her babies in early summer in Mama B's flower garden—safe in the protection of the picket fence. Mama B enjoys watching the half grown rabbits now as they play at the edge of Rabbit Run Road. Mrs. Rabbit has a hard time keeping up with her little ones as they run, jump and play. It is a full time job for her as she tries to nibble and watch for danger at the same time.

The rabbits are especially pretty now in the autumn with the extra layer of fur that nature has provided to keep them warm. Sometimes all Mama B can see are the little snow-white cotton tails as the rabbits hop down Rabbit Run Road. Then they stop and stand-
up on their back feet, with their front paws near their chest—looking, sniffing, and listening. Mrs. Rabbit has been training them to keep a watchful eye out for danger—like Bo, who enjoys nothing better than a good rabbit chase. But the rabbits have been well-taught and they run quickly into the briar patch when they see Bo coming. As for Bo, he stops on a dime at the edge of the briar patch because he knows the briars will stick him.

Down the hill and at the edge of Rabbit Run Road, high up in a persimmon tree, is an opossum eating a delicious persimmon. The persimmon tree, which lost leaves and some fruit in the hurricane, still looks festive with enough orange fruit to give it a bright color. The persimmon is a favorite food of opossums. Although the opossum travels mostly at night, he cannot resist the delicious persimmons in the early morning hours.

Bo barks and he comes running down Rabbit Run Road. He has spotted a buzzard flying overhead. Bo tries to guard the farm from creatures of the sky as well as on the ground. At the bottom of the hill, he forgets the buzzard and stops immediately. He has picked-up the scent of the opossum near the persimmon tree. Bo sniffs the base of the tree— *Yes, he has found the opossum!* There he goes—*bark, bark, bark*—as he runs around the tree. The opossum looks down at Bo with a grin, showing Bo all of his sharp white teeth. The wise old thing knows he is not in danger and continues eating the persimmons. Resigned, Bo walks slowly, back toward Bluebird Hill.

The first chill of autumn has descended on the rolling hills of south central Mississippi. The recent light frost has turned the few remaining leaves on the Bradford pear, hickory, and maple trees brilliant colors of orange, yellow and red. The leaves that were still left on the big oak tree in the yard have turned brown. They are falling steadily in a brisk north wind. Mama B is outside raking the crunchy leaves into a pile. She carries them in a large wooden basket to her flower garden. The leaves and pine straw are used as a mulch to keep her plants from freezing in the winter.

Just like the animals of Bluebird Hill, Mama B and Papa Doc have a busy autumn as they prepare for winter.

Mama B hears a familiar sound in the distance. *Ah, yes*, she thinks, *last spring*. She looks up in the blue sky where she sees the V formation of geese. They are migrating back to the coastal areas of the south and South America where they live during the winter months. They spent their summer in the northern states and Canada but when temperatures begin to drop, the geese head south to escape the cold artic wind, snow and ice.

Here comes Fritz the squirrel across the yard. Mama B saw him earlier in the edge of the pasture heading for the pecan tree. He was on a scouting mission looking for food. He has not one but two pecans in his mouth. Fritz knows autumn is a time to store food and prepare his supplies for winter meals. Mama B stands back and watches as Fritz digs a hole in the ground with his front feet and stores the pecans in the hole. He is careful to cover the pecans so another squirrel won't find them. There will be cold winter days when he does not have food and the buried food will be a wonderful dinner.

Mama B has finished raking the oak leaves and has taken down the hummingbird feeders. She is in the farmhouse washing the feeders and will put them away until the tiny birds return to Bluebird Hill in the spring. The hummingbirds flew south from Bluebird Hill in the middle of October when they sensed the change of season.

Papa Doc is checking the bluebird houses. The bluebirds will not leave the farm during autumn. They live on Bluebird Hill all year— that's how the farm got its name.

Autumn days are good working days on the farm. The temperature is in the sixties today and Papa Doc is in the mood to plant. First he cleans the summer vegetable garden spot. Then, while Mama B goes to Tylertown Farm Supply to buy seeds and plants, he breaks the ground. When all is ready, he will plant broccoli, cabbage, mustard, turnips, carrots, and onions. Papa Doc is also planting rye grass, winter wheat, and clover in the food plots for the cows and wildlife to eat in the winter. The winter grass stays green most of the winter—a treat cows particularly enjoy. The grass along with hay and tubs of protein bought at Tylertown Farm Supply should satisfy their appetites until spring.

Much of the hay had been cut before Katrina. After the hay dried on the ground it was baled. The tractor, pulling a trailer, brought the large bales of hay to Bluebird Hill. The bales of hay are placed end–to-end just outside the pasture fence. The bales are close enough to the pasture and should not be a problem for Papa Doc when he needs to move a bale inside the pasture for the cows on a rainy cold winter day.

Mama B has returned from town and is decorating the front yard and porch on Bluebird Hill with autumn decorations. She is making a scarecrow using Papa Doc's old clothes. Papa Doc is fussing a little because he is not ready to give the scarecrow the clothes Mama B is using. But Papa Doc's fussing has not changed her mind. She is not going to undress her scarecrow just to give Papa Doc his old clothes back. They are worn out and she knows he will continue to wear them, unless they are given to the scarecrow. Mama B is surrounding the scarecrow with pumpkins, gourds, corn stalks and golden yellow leaves from the hickory tree. Bluebird Hill is now officially dressed for autumn. Come to think of it, Bo is also dressed for autumn with the beautiful winter coat that is coming in so long, shiny, and thick.

Not to be outdone by Bo and the rabbits, the chickens are molting. Molting is the process of shedding and adding new feathers. Chickens and birds shed some feathers and add new ones in order to keep warm during the winter. Mama B helps too by placing fresh pine straw, still in plentiful supply since Katrina, on the dirt floor in both chicken houses to help protect the chickens' feet from the cold ground in the winter. She also closes their little window so that they will be warm and cozy.

Papa Doc is in the woods cutting up trees that were blown down or damaged by Katrina. The wood, cut in twelve inch lengths, will be used in the wood stove to keep the farmhouse warm.

A hawk flies over the farm scanning the ground for something to eat. Rufus looks up and his squawking warns all the chickens of danger above. (Hawks do love a tasty chicken now and again.) The other little roosters, Lewey, Hewey and Dewey are in rooster training and follow their Daddy's instructions with their alerts. Goldie, Cream, Sugar, and Spice stand very still until the hawk flies out of sight. *Look somewhere else, Mr. Hawk! These chickens are safe inside their fenced in chicken yard.* The hawk flies off and lands on a limb in the pecan tree at the edge of Rabbit Run Road. He watches and waits. Soon he sees Mama B coming with a bucket in her hand. She stops under the pecan tree and starts to pick up pecans. The hawk flies to a nearby tree and watches. The big bird does not give up easily. He will return to his perch in the pecan tree as soon as Mama B is gone.

Papa Doc and Bo are waiting for Mama B on the back porch when she returns with the pecans. Soon Papa Doc is cracking the pecans with the pecan cracker and Mama B is picking out the meat. Mama B would love to give Fritz some of the delicious pecan meat but Papa Doc says the cracking and picking is far too much work to give to a squirrel.

It's very early on a chilly morning when Fritz is awakened by the sound of Mama B driving off in the pick-up truck. Just the day before, she was gone a very long time. He saw her return with bags and bags of groceries and then she was busy in the kitchen all the rest of the day. *So where is she off to now?*

Mama B is on her way to the animal shelter. As she approaches the entrance, she notices a new banner hanging across the gate welcoming visitors. It is the week of Thanksgiving and many Best Friends volunteers from all over the country have returned to Mississippi for a Thanksgiving weekend reunion. It is to be a joyous occasion because so many of the animals have been adopted into loving homes. A whole new group of volunteers has just arrived to work at the shelter. Even after three months, many animals still need to be rescued from the storm-ravaged areas of the Gulf Coast. Mama B wants to be part of the celebration by bringing the workers a special treat on this special day when there is so much to be thankful for. For this occasion, she has prepared one hundred and fifty turkey cookies made from chocolate cream filled cookies.

Fritz is still on the look-out when Mama B returns and rushes back into the farmhouse kitchen. Soon the sound of a car coming down the gravel road has Fritz's attention. The car comes to a stop under his big oak tree and two small children scramble out and race off to the tire swing while their parents head for the farmhouse.

Grandchildren, Katie and Austin Cole, have arrived. Austin had promised his little sister Katie that she could have the first ride on the swing. Austin sticks to his word and is doing a good job as pusher. The higher Katie goes in the air, the louder she squeals. And the louder she squeals, the more jittery Fritz becomes. After all, he thinks the swing belongs to him since it hangs on a limb of his oak tree.

Now Fritz sees another car approaching. There are older children and grown-ups getting out of the car with duffle bags. Fritz gets a little closer so that he can get a better look. There is Alex, Madison and Graham and they waste no time in joining Katie and Austin Cole. Fritz hears laughter coming from the farmhouse. The laughter is a sign of happiness and Fritz knows Mama B is happy because she has most of her grandchildren on Bluebird Hill.

Curious Fritz, the unusual squirrel with the unusual name, is wondering why all the people are on Bluebird Hill. He can see Mama B thru the glass door of the farmhouse where she is busy cooking and chatting happily with her family. She has placed a pecan pie on the back porch to cool. The children slamming the farmhouse door and the happy voices coming from inside have attracted the attention of all the animals on Bluebird Hill. Mama B is standing in the kitchen holding a tray filled with a flock of tiny turkeys. *Of course, she made some extra cookies for her grandchildren.*

After a blessing of thanks, the big Thanksgiving feast is enjoyed by all the family on Bluebird Hill. Papa Doc especially savored the pecan pie. The children have Thanksgiving turkey cookies in their mouths, on their hands, and on their minds as they ask if they can take the extras home.

Another Thanksgiving has come and gone. This holiday marks the end of an autumn season that is one for the history books. When Mama B and Papa Doc reflect back on all that has happened, they try to remember that in spite of the tragedy that the storm brought, there was good too—the good people who came from everywhere to help, those who sent supplies, those who prayed. Even Papa Doc's beloved oak trees that were felled by Katrina, were put to

good use to warm the farmhouse. As she reflects over this autumn, Mama B sees a special kind of grace and goodness in the return of the birds with their sweet songs reminding her that life goes on as another season arrives on Bluebird Hill.

As they stand by the wood stove warming their hands they realize winter has arrived on Bluebird Hill. Papa Doc says… "Do we have marshmallows for a cup of hot chocolate." (another must for him - if it gets down to 55 degrees it is a GOTTA HAVE.)

The End

RECIPES

Have fun making a flock of chocolate turkeys!

1 Bag Chocolate Cream filled cookies

1 Can Chocolate Cake Frosting

1 Small Bag Malted Milk Balls

1 Bag Candy Corn

1 Bag Red Cinnamon Candy

Note: For one turkey you will use 1 cream filled cookie, a little frosting, 3 candy corn, 1 malted milk ball and 1 red cinnamon candy.

Pull apart one cookie. Scrape all white cream icing from one side of cookie and spread on the other cookie.

Place cookie with icing, icing side up on a paper plate. Place one malt ball in center of cookie.

Spread chocolate icing on remaining cookie. Holding back of cookie with your fingers on each side, stand cookie on its side and press chocolate icing side against malt ball on paper plate.

Place 3 candy corn at the top of standing up cookie to form colorful tail feathers. The corn is placed with small end pointing toward malt ball.

Using a little chocolate frosting stick red cinnamon candy on top of malt ball for turkey head. You have just finished one turkey. Now, complete your flock. Let the turkey cookies set overnight and they will become firm enough to handle.

More favorite desserts of the animal shelter volunteers.

CHESS SQUARES

Preheat oven 350 degrees.

MIX together 1 egg, 1 box yellow cake mix and 1 stick margarine (room temperature). Press into bottom of 9 x 13 inch pan that has been sprayed with cooking spray.

BEAT together 2 eggs, 1 - 8 ounce package cream cheese (room temperature), 1 box confectioners sugar, 1 teaspoon vanilla extract and 1/2 teaspoon almond extract.

POUR the second mixture over the cake mix mixture. Place on center rack of oven and bake at 350 degrees for 40 minutes or until brown on top. Cool before cutting into squares.

FUDGE CAKE

1 box Devil's Food Cake Mix baked as per package in 13 x 9 inch pan.

FROSTING:
2 Cups Sugar
1/2 Cup Whole Milk
1/2 Cup Cocoa
1 Stick Margarine (or butter)
1 Teaspoon Vanilla Extract
1 Cup Chopped Pecans (optional)

Mix first four ingredients together in a medium saucepan. Bring to a hard boil and boil for one minute. Take off heat and add vanilla and pecans. Place pan in cold water and beat until thick enough to spread on cake. (if it gets too thick… add a little more milk.)

PINEAPPLE FROSTED OR FILLED CAKE

Using your favorite cake mix, bake as directed on package and frost or fill with this sticky, gooey, yummy delight.

1 Box Yellow (or other favorite) Cake Mix baked as per package in 13 x 9 inch pan.

FROSTING/FILLING:
3 Tablespoons all-purpose Flour
1/2 Cup Granulated Sugar
1 (20-ounce) Can crushed Pineapple (do not drain)
2 Tablespoons Butter or Margarine
1 Teaspoon Lemon Juice

COMBINE flour and sugar in a small saucepan; add pineapple, butter and lemon juice. Cook over medium heat, stirring constantly, until thickened. Cool and spread on your favorite cake.

TEA CAKES

(preheat oven to 400 degrees)
1 Cup Butter or Margarine
1 1/4 Cups Granulated Sugar
3 Eggs
3 Cups All Purpose Flour
1 Teaspoon Baking Powder
1/4 Teaspoon Salt
1 Teaspoon Vanilla Extract

Cream butter and sugar until light; add eggs, one at a time and beat after each. Add baking powder, salt and vanilla at once; beat well. Gradually add flour and mix well.

Roll out on floured board 1/4- inch thick and cut into desired shape. Place on lightly greased cookie sheet. Bake (center rack) 400 degrees 12 minutes or untily lightly browned. Remove immediately from pan and cool on wire rack. Approximately 4 dozen cookies to enjoy.

Enjoy!
From the Kitchen of Mama B

If you are interested in helping either of these two wonderful organizations, through a donation or by volunteering, here is how to contact them.

Best Friends Animal Society
5001 Angel Canyon Road
Kanab, Utah 84741-5000
(435) 644-2001

St. Francis Animal Sanctuary
P. O. Box 677
Abita Springs, Louisiana 70420
(601) 222-1927